Caring For RABBIT

by Marianne Mays

The DALMATIAN PRESS name and logo are
trademarks of Dalmatian Press, LLC, Franklin, Tennessee 37067.
No part of this book may be reproduced or copied in any form
without the written permission of Dalmatian Press, LLC.
Editor *Mary Ginder*
Designer *Dan Waters*
ISBN: 1-40370-887-8

13471 Caring For Your Rabbit
04 05 06 07 08 WWP 10 9 8 7 6 5 4 3 2 1

About the Author

Marianne Mays is an experienced breeder and exhibitor and has kept rabbits for many years. She has cared for a variety of different breeds, but she has specialized in Cashmere Lops and Polish. Marianne has owned two Silver Star Diploma winners, and has supplied winning stock to breeders in Britain and Scandinavia. She has contributed to numerous specialist magazines on small livestock, and has edited a number of club magazines and journals.

Marianne, a qualified veterinary nurse, was born in Sweden and now lives in England with her husband, Nick, who is a specialist in all areas of keeping small livestock. They have two children, and share their home with a variety of pets, including Golden Retrievers, rabbits, and pedigree cats, which they breed and show.

Acknowledgements

Many thanks to Shaun Flannery, Lol Middleton, John Symonds, and my husband, Nick, for the photographs; to Sheridan and Stephanie Smith for being such excellent models; to the Doncaster Excelsior Fur Society for letting us photograph rabbits at one of their shows; to the management and staff of Jolleys Pet Superstore, Doncaster, for allowing their stock to be photographed; and last, but not least, to my good friend Linda Dykes for much advice on rabbits and rabbit-keeping over the years.

Contents

Diarrhea ("Scours")
Intestinal Blockages and Hairballs
Bloat
Malocclusion
Myxomatosis
Rabbit Viral Hemorrhagic Disease

INTRODUCING THE RABBIT

Rabbits and humans have a long history together, though the notion of rabbits as pets, especially house pets, is relatively recent. Although rabbits were "officially" discovered by the Phoenicians, the great seafaring traders of the ancient world, circa 1100 BC, it's likely that rabbits were around long before they made it into the historical record.

Rabbits originated in southwestern Europe and northwestern Africa, but were traded around the world by the Phoenicians and then later the Romans. In the Roman Empire, rabbits were kept in enclosures called *Leporaria* so that they could be drawn upon as a convenient food source. The rabbit must have been important in Roman eyes, for it was depicted on coins issued during the reign of the Emperor Hadrian in the years 120–130 AD.

The popularity of rabbits as pets has led to a huge development in the number of breeds.

This rabbit is a Siamese Smoke Netherland Dwarf.

The Normans brought several specimens from Europe to the
British Isles after their conquest in 1066. Rabbits were a form
of livestock, living in enclosures and warrens (burrows) in a
semi-captive state, so that they could be easily obtained for
food. This practice continued for centuries.

Development of Rabbits as Pets

During the 1830s and 1840s, various enthusiasts in Britain—
mainly farmers and landowners—began to develop specialized
breeds of rabbits. One of the first was the English Lop, with its
lengthy ear span. In America, pet rabbits did not capture much
public interest until after 1900. The Belgian Hare was one of
the first popular breeds in the U.S. and its success encouraged
the development of many new breeds.

Rabbit clubs grew increasingly popular. The National Pet Stock
Association was formed in 1910 and, over time, evolved into

*There is evidence that a long-haired
Angora breed was developed during
the Roman Empire.*

The American Rabbit
Breeders Association
(ARBA). The ARBA
has more than
30,000 members and
many affiliated clubs
throughout the
United States. Its
stated mission is the
"promotion, develop-
ment, and improve-
ment of the domes-
tic rabbit and cavy
[guinea pig]."

Is a Rabbit the Right Pet for You?

It's easy to fall in love with a cute little bunny at the pet store, but you need to know more about what rabbits are like as pets before you decide to bring one home. Rabbits are social creatures and can be very affectionate, but they would rather be petted or have their heads scratched than sit on your lap and be held. Consider the following questions carefully.

1. WHO IS GOING TO BE RESPONSIBLE FOR THE RABBIT?
A rabbit is a living animal that will need care throughout its life, which is likely to be 7–9 years long. It is not a toy to discard when the novelty has worn off. Children under the age of 12 usually need assistance with pet care and cannot be expected to take full responsibility. Are you willing to take care of the pet should the child lose interest in it?

2. DO YOU HAVE OTHER PETS?
Rabbits are a prey species. To cats and dogs, they look like something to be hunted. While some families are successful in integrating rabbits with other pets, there are obviously some risks involved. Even small dogs and cats are powerful

Rabbits are a wonderful choice for a family pet, though they are not well-suited for very young children. The rabbit has strong hind legs which are capable of hurting a child who is not yet strong enough to handle the rabbit properly. For children under seven, a guinea pig may be a better choice.

This pair may never become the best of friends, but with time and attention on your part, they may learn to tolerate each other.

Rabbits and dogs do not have to be enemies. However, the dog must be well trained, and you must always supervise sessions when they are together.

enough to kill your rabbit, even if they seem to be getting along. If you are willing to take the time to introduce the pets gradually and with strict supervision, rabbits can live in a household with cats or dogs. Even when the animals appear to be used to each other, you'll still need to oversee their time together.

3. **WHERE WILL THE RABBIT BE HOUSED?**
Traditionally, rabbits have been housed in outdoor hutches. In recent years, however, this practice has been criticized by pet experts and organizations like the Humane Society of the United States. Even in a wire cage, rabbits are not completely safe from predators such as raccoons, owls, cats, and dogs. Rabbits are greatly frightened when they sense a predator nearby, even if it cannot get to them. If a rabbit panics, there's a good chance it will injure itself. Other "outdoor" threats include pesticides, insect-borne illnesses, and humans who might want to harm or steal the animal,

Rabbits are very social animals and do not thrive if left alone in their cages for extended periods of time. The majority of pet rabbits can be litter trained, particularly if they have been altered (spayed or neutered). As with any other type of animal kept in the house, the litter box and cage will need to be kept clean to prevent odors.

Do you have enough space in your home for a cage and for the rabbit to exercise when not in the cage? The cage should be about five times the size of the rabbit, with room inside for a food dish, litter box, and bedding. Do you have one or more rooms which could be made "bunny-proof," allowing your rabbit to play and exercise safely?

Some owners house their rabbits in a shed or outbuilding, but do not keep a rabbit in a garage—fuel fumes and carbon monoxide can be deadly. Outdoor hutches are safest from predators in yards that are fenced in. Also, rabbits do not tolerate extreme temperatures, especially heat, so make sure the outdoor hutch is protected from the weather and not in direct sun.

4. **CAN YOU AFFORD TO PROVIDE GOOD CARE?**
In addition to the routine costs of providing adequate housing and good nutrition, you should plan to spay or neuter

your pet (this has numerous benefits beyond preventing unwanted offspring). Other vet care will also be necessary and can be more expensive than caring for a more common pet like a cat or dog.

Where to Buy a Rabbit

Most people visit their local pet shop to buy a rabbit. This works well if the pet shop is a good one with knowledgeable staff and all you want is a nice pet. However, visiting a rabbit breeder does have advantages. A breeder will be able to sell you a rabbit of the exact breed that you want, while pet shops may offer a limited number of breeds or only cross-breeds. A local rabbit club or an Internet search will be able to help you locate rabbit breeders in your area.

A breeder will also be able to tell you a rabbit's exact date of birth, show you its parents, and tell you what the rabbit is used to eating. This gives you a sense not only of the rabbit's size when full-grown, but also its likely temperament. If the parents are nice and friendly, chances are that your rabbit will be, too.

How Many Rabbits?

Rabbits are social animals by nature and often enjoy living in pairs rather than alone. However, you will only want to raise two rabbits together if both have been neutered. In addition to the obvious reason for this—to prevent unwanted and numerous offspring—altering the animals reduces much of their natural tendencies to be aggressive or defend their territory. Neutered male-female pairs usually work the best. In fact, brother-sister pairs can also be raised and kept together if neutered at an early age.

It is important to introduce rabbits to each other gradually and see if they get along, particularly if you already have one rabbit at home and are adding another. Sometimes they seem to "fall in love" and develop a very strong bond, while other pairs do not get along at all. Some breeders and rescue organizations will let you bring your pet rabbit in to see which of their rabbits it finds easiest to get along with.

Selecting a Healthy Rabbit

1. **AGE:** A rabbit should not be sold under the age of six weeks. Smaller breeds, such as the Netherland Dwarf, can leave their mother for a new home at the age of six weeks, but larger breeds, such as the French Lop, often need a little longer to mature, so they are best left until the age of eight to nine weeks.

2. **BEHAVIOR:** The rabbit should be lively and curious. It should not be frightened or listless.

3. **EARS:** Ears should be clean and free from any crustiness inside or outside. The ears on a very young rabbit of a lop breed may not have lopped (drooped to the sides) by six to eight weeks of age, so don't be surprised if the ears are still somewhat upright. This is normal—the ears should lop by the age of twelve weeks.

4. **NOSE:** The nose should be clean with no discharge, and there must be no evidence of sneezing.

5. **TAIL AREA:** The tail and surrounding areas should be clean and dry, with no sign of diarrhea or staining.

6. **FUR:** The fur should be soft and dense, and free from mites or dirt. A longhaired rabbit may have a slightly bald neck as a youngster because the baby fur does not cover the body as well as the adult fur does. A shorthaired breed should have no bare patches at all.

7. **FEET:** The rabbit's feet should be clean. If the fur on the inside of the front legs is matted, it's a sign that the rabbit has been using its front legs to wipe a runny nose. The claws should be short and sharp on youngsters (overgrown claws suggest that the rabbit is a mature one).

8. **BODY:** The whole body should be firm and even. It must not be too thin, or have an extended pot belly, which may indicate the presence of worms or some form of disease.

Even rabbits that appear healthy should be checked by your vet soon after being purchased.

Sexing Rabbits

Baby rabbits need to be four or five weeks old before it is possible to determine their gender—and even then it's easy to make a mistake. Large breeds are slightly easier to sex than smaller ones, simply because their genitalia are larger.

The easiest way of determining the sex of a young rabbit is to place the rabbit on its back on the palm of one of your hands. Make sure that you have a good grip—small rabbits can jump surprisingly well. With the other hand, gently press with two fingers around the sexual organ. A small opening will then be visible. In the male (the buck), this will look like a circle; in the female (the doe) the opening will be V-shaped.

If all the youngsters examined appear to have circular openings, it may be because they are still too young to be sexed properly. If this is the case, wait a week and try again. If you still get the same result, then you can safely assume that they are all bucks. It is much easier to sex an adult rabbit. An adult buck will have two fairly large testicles that are clearly visible. The doe will have a large V-shaped opening.

Colors and Markings

To understand the descriptions of the various breeds which follow, you need to know the way that colors are categorized.

AGOUTI: The natural brown-gray color, as seen in wild rabbits.
BLACK: As dense black as possible. The underfur is normally a blue-gray tone.
WHITE: Pure white, with either red or blue eyes.
SOOTY FAWN: Also known as **TORTOISESHELL**, this is an orange/brown top color, with underfur of a blue tone. The sides of the rabbit, as well as the face, ears, legs, feet and tail, are shaded in a dark-gray color.
FAWN OR YELLOW: A bright fawn color with pale, almost white, underfur. The rabbit's stomach is white.
BLUE: An even blue-gray.
CHOCOLATE: An even, warm brown.
LILAC: Dove gray.
CHINCHILLA: This is a version of the agouti coloration in which

all-brown pigmentation has been replaced by white. The rabbit has a dark-blue under-color, white middle-color, and each hair is tipped with black, giving the rabbit an overall impression of silver.

SIAMESE SMOKE: Also known as **SMOKE PEARL** and **BLUE SABLE**. The color is blue-gray with a darker gray on the rabbit's sides, face, ears, legs, feet, and tail.

SIAMESE SABLE: In some countries this is known as BROWN **SABLE**. It is the brown version of Siamese smoke. The rabbit is brown, with the shade varying from light to very dark. The sides, ears, face, legs, feet, and tail are very dark-gray.

SEALPOINT: Also known as **SIAMESE**. The color is like the Sealpoint Siamese cat, although the eyes are not blue. The rabbit is of a beige to gray color, with dark-gray face, ears, legs, feet, and tail. The amount of dark shading can vary— some rabbits have shading confined to the lower sides of their body, others have a dark-gray color all over.

TAN PATTERN: This is a black, blue, chocolate, or lilac rabbit with a rich tan-colored belly.

OTTER: Basically the same as tan, although the rabbit's underside is pale beige with tan-colored borders.

FOX: A colored rabbit with a white underside.

STEEL: A much darker version of the agouti.

HIMALAYAN: A pure white rabbit with a colored smut (spot) on the nose, and colored ears, legs, feet, and tail. The eyes are always red.

BROKEN MARKED OR BUTTERFLY: A white rabbit with colored markings: a colored butterfly-shaped smut (spot) on the nose, colored patches around the eyes, colored ears, a large colored mantle on the back, and other spotting.

UNWANTED RABBITS
Consider adopting a rabbit from a shelter or animal rescue organization. Thousands each year are euthanized because their owners no longer wanted to care for them. This is particularly true after the Easter holidays when giving baby rabbits to children is so popular. Should you ever decide to get rid of a your pet rabbit, be sure to find a good home for it or take it to a reputable shelter or rescue. Never release it into the "wild"— it has no protection and will soon be killed.

Popular Rabbit Breeds

Some breeds make better pets than others. It is hard to generalize, however, since most rabbits are bred for appearance traits rather than for temperament. Rabbits are also individuals with unique personalities, some being friendlier or more tolerant than others. Early handling makes a big difference, too—rabbits that are not handled often and gently right from the start are less likely to be easy-going and affectionate pets.

The American Rabbit Breeders Association (ARBA) currently sanctions (recognizes) the following rabbit breeds. There are many other breeds available and breeders are always working to develop new ones. If you have heard of a rabbit breed which is not listed below, you'll probably find information about it easily with an Internet search. There are a lot of rabbits available that are cross-breeds or mongrels, and these are just as likely as pure-breds to make wonderful pets. You don't need a pure-bred rabbit unless you intend to show it or breed it.

If you are looking for a pet and not for a show rabbit, a cross-breed will do just fine.

The breeds are listed here by size, which is not to imply that any size is particularly the best for a pet owner. Some of the small breeds can be a bit too temperamental as pets unless you are an experienced rabbit owner. On the other hand, some of the giant breeds are very docile and make wonderful pets, though they do require more space.

Small (6 lbs or less when full grown)
AMERICAN FUZZY LOP
The American Fuzzy Lop is a fairly new breed. It is a lot like a Holland Lop rabbit, but with a long woolly coat.

BRITANNIA PETITE

In other countries, this breed is known as the Polish rabbit, but since there was already a Polish rabbit breed in America when they were imported, the British Polish rabbit was renamed the Britannia Petite. It is the breed from which the Netherland Dwarf was originated. (The name Polish does not refer to Poland, but to the rabbit's glossy coat which looks like it has been polished.)

Britannia Petite

The Britannia Petite is a small, slender rabbit, with long legs. It tends to be high-spirited and jumpy so this breed is recommended for experienced rabbit owners and not for young children. This breed has short fur and comes in a variety of colors.

DUTCH

Perhaps the best-known rabbit breed, Dutch rabbits have a distinctive look. The head and ears are colored, with a white blaze (stripe) in the middle. The front part of the body is white and the second half of the body is colored. The Dutch rabbit comes in several different colors, such as black, blue, chocolate, yellow, and tortoiseshell. The Dutch rabbit makes an ideal pet.

Blue Dutch

Black Dutch

DWARF HOTOT

Dwarf Hotot (pronounced *ho-toe*) rabbits are popular due to their friendly disposition, playfulness, and sociability. The ideal Dwarf Hotot for showing is a white rabbit with short ears and black bands circling the eyes. Since this breed is still being developed, other markings sometimes occur.

FLORIDA WHITE
These small, round white rabbits with bright pink eyes were developed as meat animals and for use in laboratories. They are easy to care for and are popular with show exhibitors.

HAVANA
Havanas are descended from the Dutch breed and are known for their laid-back temperament and the minklike texture of their fur. They are not as active as many other breeds and tend to be docile pets. Havanas can be black, chocolate, or blue.

Havana

HIMALAYAN
A fairly small, slender rabbit with red eyes and a white body. It has a colored face, ears, feet, and tail, which can be black, blue, chocolate, or lilac. With their loving personality and small size, they make great pets.

Black Himalayan

HOLLAND LOP
The Holland Lop is a very popular breed for pet owners as well as exhibitors. It comes in a great variety of colors, such as white, black, blue, agouti, chinchilla, Siamese, sable, smoke, sealpoint, fawn, sooty-fawn, etc. When showing, they are usually divided into two groups: Solid and Broken markings (spotted). Holland Lops are playful and active—a good choice for first-time owners.

Holland Lop

JERSEY WOOLY
The Jersey Wooly was developed in the 1980s by an American breeder who wanted to produce small rabbits with long but easy-to-groom hair (wool). Jersey Woolys are calm enough to make good pets for families with young children.

MINI LOP
Also known as the German Lop, these little rabbits are friendly and intelligent. They require less grooming than longer-haired breeds. Mini Lops enjoy plenty of exercise and interaction.

Mini Lop

MINI REX
Mini Rex rabbits weigh about 4 lbs and have short, velvety fur like the standard Rex rabbits. They are a good choice for kids.

NETHERLAND DWARF
The Netherland Dwarf is a very small rabbit, weighing no more than 2 lbs. It has very short ears that are less than two inches long and a round body and face. Colors include white, black, blue, Siamese sable, smoke pearl, sealpoint, opal, tan, chinchilla, etc. Netherland Dwarfs are very active and need lots of attention, room to play, and toys to play with. Some of them are prone to biting, though this can be reduced by spaying or neutering them. Temperament is largely inherited, so try to handle the rabbit's parents and see if they are good-natured.

White Netherland Dwarf

Siamese Smoke Netherland Dwarf

POLISH (AMERICAN POLISH)
Polish rabbits are known for their great personality and also for their hardiness, being adaptable to a wide range of climates and needing little in the way of special diet or handling. They should not be confused with the English breed called Polish (which is known as the "Britannia Petite" breed in the U.S.).

SILVER
This is a rabbit with a sparkling appearance due to its even covering of silver hairs. There are four colors: black (known as the Silver Gray), blue (Silver Blue), fawn (Silver Fawn) and brown (Silver Brown). Silvers make sweet-tempered pets.

TAN
This is an attractive rabbit with distinctive shiny markings. It has a colored body, which can be black, blue, chocolate, or lilac, with a belly and underside of a rich, deep tan. Tans are an old breed relative to many of the

Blue Tan

others, dating back to the 19th century. They make good pets. Tans are inquisitive and active, and benefit from having larger cages so they can move around as much as they need to.

Medium (6 to 9 lbs when full grown)

AMERICAN SABLE
This is a breed known for its calm temperament as well as its beauty. The color is a dark sepia brown on the back, face, legs and tail, gradually becoming paler over the rest of the body. They can be either marten sable (with a white under-side) or Siamese sable

Siamese Sable

(without the white underside). This breed makes a good pet and is an excellent choice for young people getting started as exhibitors.

BELGIAN HARE

As the name suggests, the rabbit looks like a wild hare, with a long body, long legs, and long ears. The color is usually red, with blotchy ticking across the body. They are very active and require large cages with room to run around as well as solid

Belgian Hare

(not wire) floors to protect their feet. Most are easy to handle and they can develop strong bonds with their owners.

ENGLISH ANGORA

One of four Angora breeds, the English Angora is the smallest, weighing about 6 lbs. It comes in many colors, including golden, cream, blue, lilac, chocolate, smoke, white, etc. The fur should be as long as possible and cover the whole rabbit, complete with large tufts of fur on the ears. They have a good personality as pets, but require extensive grooming.

Angora

ENGLISH SPOT (ENGLISH RABBIT)

The English Spot is a white rabbit with colored spots, colored ears, color around the eyes, and a so-called colored smut (spot) on the nose. There is an

English Spot

unbroken line of color along the spine. The English Spot comes in black, blue, tortoiseshell, chocolate, lilac, and gray. It makes a friendly and loving pet.

FRENCH ANGORA
French Angora rabbits can be white or colored, including Broken pattern (spotted). They require less grooming than the English Angora which makes them somewhat easier for some owners to manage as a pet.

HARLEQUIN
(JAPANESE RABBIT)
One side of the head is black, the other orange, and the body is striped in bands of the two colors. Colors include black, blue, chocolate, and lilac. Harlequins make ideal pets, as they are social and easy to care for.

Harlequin

LILAC
Lilac rabbits have very silky, dove-gray coats with a hint of a pinkish tint. They are another good choice for pet owners.

REX
A Rex rabbit completely lacks coarse guard hairs in its fur, having only the very soft underfur. The result is a soft, velvetlike coat which is very dense. Rex rabbits are friendly and well-suited for pet owners. They come in colors such as white (known as the Ermine Rex), black,

Castor Rex

blue, lilac, Havana, smoke pearl, agouti (known as Castor Rex), sable, sealpoint, fox, tan, Dalmatian (spotted like the dog), harlequin, tri-color, etc.

RHINELANDER

With their dramatic tri-color patterns, Rhinelanders are some-times called the "Calico" of rabbit breeds. They have white base color with black and gold markings, including a saddle marking and a "butterfly" mark on their faces.

SATIN ANGORA

Hollow wool fibers in their coat give a shiny appearance which makes these rabbits look like they have a satin finish. They have a quiet temperament, but, as with any Angora breed, Satin Angoras require extensive grooming.

SILVER MARTEN

The Silver Marten resulted from crossing Tan and Standard Chinchilla breeds. The ARBA recognizes four varieties: black, blue, chocolate, and sable. They make fine pets, but are good at escaping and at jumping from high places.

STANDARD CHINCHILLA

A very pretty rabbit, the Standard Chinchilla is a popu-lar pet, being both intelligent and docile. The color gives an overall sil-ver impression.

Chinchilla

Large (9 to 11 lbs when full grown)

AMERICAN

The American rabbit comes in two colors: Blue (slate blue coat, blue eyes) and White (with pink eyes). They make calm pets.

AMERICAN CHINCHILLA

This breed was developed from the Standard Chinchilla type to produce a larger, meatier rabbit. They need to be groomed reg-ularly to keep their coats in good condition.

BEVEREN

Although still fairly rare in the United States, the Beveren is an old breed, well-known in Europe. This breed is most often found in blue, but it also comes in white, black, brown, and lilac. With a weight of at least 8 lbs, it will make a good pet if the owner has room for a fairly large rabbit.

CALIFORNIAN
This breed is similar to the Himalayan, but with a rounder, meatier body. It has a white body with colored face, ears, feet, and tail. Californian rabbits are usually gentle and friendly.

CHAMPAGNE D'ARGENT
This breed was developed in the Champagne area of France at least a century ago. "Argente" is the French word for silver; and though these rabbits are black at birth, they develop a silver color as they mature.

CINNAMON
This is a lovely rabbit for pet owners or for exhibitors. The coat is cinnamon brown, with orange undercolor and gray ticking.

CREME D'ARGENT
The Creme type is similar to the Champagne d'Argent rabbit, but smaller. Their cream-colored coats are slightly tinted with orange. Like the Champagne d'Argent, these are rather rare.

ENGLISH LOP
This is the original Lop breed and is longer and more slender than the other Lops. The ears, measured from the tip of one ear to the tip of the other, can be as much as 28 inches long. The English Lop needs a large hutch, so it can move around easily and avoid treading on its

English Lop

delicate ears. It is friendly, but best left to the experienced rabbit keeper. Colors include black, fawn, sooty-fawn, and agouti.

GIANT ANGORA
With long wool that requires extensive grooming, the Giant Angora may not be the best choice for pet owners, though they are usually quite easy-going.

HOTOT
(BLANC DE HOTOT)

A distinctive rabbit, pure white with dark eyes and black "spectacles" around the eyes. It is named after the area in France where it was developed and is still rare in the U.S.

Hotot

NEW ZEALAND

This is a large and round rabbit originally developed for meat and fur. The color is usually white, but they also come in black, blue, and red. The New Zealand has a nice personality.

Red New Zealand

White New Zealand

PALOMINO

This breed was created to be commercial meat rabbits, but their gentle and friendly personalities make them good pets. They come in golden and lynx color varieties.

SATIN

Satins are very attractive rabbits with sparkling coats. The ARBA recognizes these colors: black, blue, broken, Californian, chinchilla, chocolate, copper, otter group, red, Siamese, and white. Satins make good pets, although their size (8–10 lbs) may make them difficult for children to handle well.

TO LEARN MORE ABOUT ANY OF THESE BREEDS

Go to the ARBA website at http://www.arba.net to see pictures of the recognized breeds and to link to member clubs.

SILVER FOX
This breed was developed in the 1920s by an American breeder who wanted a rabbit the size of a Checkered Giant but with a silver coat. Silver Fox rabbits are easy to handle and are sweet-tempered.

Black Silver Fox

Giant (11 lbs or more when full grown)

CHECKERED GIANT
In addition to their unique markings, Checkered Giants are known for being an exceptionally graceful rabbit despite their large size (around 11 lbs). They can be good pets, provided they are regularly handled and given sufficient attention.

FLEMISH GIANT
A sandy color is the most common, but Flemish Giants can also be gray, fawn, or white. They are often called the "gentle giant" of the rabbit breeds and make for hardy pets, if you can handle a pet of this size and provide adequate housing.

FRENCH LOP
The French Lop is the giant of the Lop breeds, weighing in at 10 pounds or more. Its ears are not as long as the English Lop's. It comes in colors such as agouti, black, broken-marked, chinchilla, and sooty-fawn. French Lops are a popular choice for pet owners despite their large size. They are fun to play with and don't need frequent grooming although they do require large housing with room for stretching and moving.

GIANT CHINCHILLA
The giant version of the Chinchilla weighs in at an average of 16 pounds. They have the same affectionate personality as the Standard Chinchilla and are gentle, playful pets.

2

SETTING UP:
HOUSING AND ACCESSORIES

It is a good idea to purchase all the equipment needed for a pet rabbit before you bring your new pet home. A rabbit will need peace and quiet to settle in during the first few days in a new home. This is more easily achieved if everything is ready for the rabbit on its arrival.

Housing

The single most important piece of equipment that your rabbit will need is a cage or hutch to live in. Rabbits have been kept in wooden hutches, traditionally, though all-wire metal cages have become more common in recent years, particularly for rabbits that live indoors.

THE OUTSIDE HUTCH

A hutch that is going to be located outside must be weatherproofed and able to withstand rain, snow, and wind, as well as hot and sunny weather. The outdoor hutch must be made of wood, since either metal or plastic will become too cold in the winter and too hot in summer. The best type is made of heavy, tongue-and-groove wood. A plywood hutch does not offer sufficient protection against cold weather and is not going to be durable in the long run. If you intend to keep your rabbit outside, spend a little more money on a well-made, weather-proof hutch that will serve you and your rabbit well for many years.

The outdoor hutch must be treated with wood preserver or it will eventually begin to rot. Some hutches come pre-treated, and this will be made clear by the manufacturer. If you are treating the hutch yourself, the preserver you use must be

non-toxic to animals. A hutch will usually need a new coat
of preserver every few years to keep it in good condition.
Remember to treat the inside as well as the outside.

The best type of outdoor hutch will have a separate sleeping
compartment or a partly-covered front. This is necessary so
that the rabbit can take extra shelter during bad weather. About
one-third of the front of the hutch should be covered, with the
rest being made of tough wire. Never use a hutch that has flim-
sy chicken wire as a front, because it will not be strong enough
to protect your rabbit from stray cats, dogs, or other predators.

The roof of the outside hutch is very important—it should
either be sloping (preferably with a slight overhang in the
front) or peaked. In this way, no water can gather on top of the
hutch. The roof should be covered with roofing felt or tar
paper, since treating it with wood preserver alone will not be
enough to keep it leak-proof.

If your hutch doesn't have legs, use bricks or cement blocks to
raise the hutch at least a few inches off the ground. This keeps
the hutch warmer and makes it easier for you to clean out. It
also prevents the base from rotting due to dampness. Ideally,
an outside hutch should be placed with its back against a
house or outbuilding for maximum protection. Make sure that
it is steady and cannot fall over. In very bad weather, the front
of the hutch can be covered with a tarp, as long as the covering
does not restrict the rabbit's air supply.

THE INDOOR HUTCH
This can be more simply constructed than an outside hutch.
Plywood is suitable, although it is still a good idea to treat it
with a non-toxic wood preserver to stop the rabbit's urine from
seeping into the wood, and to prolong the life of the hutch.
The front can be all wire and the roof can be flat. Ideally, the

This is an outdoor hutch appropriate in size for a single rabbit. The hutch is raised slightly off the ground and it has been treated with a wood preserver. The sloping, felted roof ensures that rain flows off the hutch and not inside it.

The separate sleeping compartment is covered to provide maximum warmth and comfort.

This is a basic wire cage with a plastic base, suitable for indoor use with a single small rabbit.

hutch is slightly raised off the ground, or placed on an old table, so you can clean it without having to kneel on the floor. A separate sleeping compartment is not necessary.

THE INDOOR CAGE
An indoor cage should have a plastic bottom tray with a wire canopy. This type of cage is easy to clean and keep free of odor. Prices vary according to the features installed in the cage.

Recommended Features

For the sake of convenience and safety, some extra features are well worth considering:

A LITTER BOARD: This is a long piece of wood placed at the front of a rabbit hutch. Ideally it should be removable and not attached to the hutch door. The litter board prevents wood shavings and other bedding from falling out of the hutch.

ANTI-CHEW DEVICES: These are pieces of tough plastic, placed on the inside of the rabbit hutch, to prevent the rabbit from chewing the wood portions.

ACCESS: If the hutch has a separate sleeping compartment, check that the opening between the bedroom and the main hutch is not too small. Avoid openings that consist of a single round hole and opt for the type that looks more like a door. If the rabbit has to jump through a hole, it may injure itself.

FRONT OPENING: The front door can swing up, down, to the right, to the left, or be completely removable. Doors that swing down, however, may be awkward when you are cleaning out.

How Big Should the Hutch Be?

Plan for a hutch that's four or five times as big as your rabbit. As a general guideline, a hutch for a small or medium-sized breed, such as a Netherland Dwarf or a Dutch, should be no smaller than 24 inches by 24 inches. For a larger breed, such as a New Zealand, a hutch 36 inches by 24 inches will be necessary. The giant breeds, such as the French Lop, need a minimum of 48 inches by 24 inches.

If you are buying a very active type of rabbit or you intend to leave the rabbit in the cage much of the time, you will be doing

The litter board aids with safety and clean-up.

the rabbit a favor by purchasing the largest cage you can afford and have room for. The height of the cage is also important. The rabbit must be able to stand up on its hind legs without touching the roof of the hutch with its head.

Furnishing the Hutch

Once you buy the housing, you will need bedding, a bowl for food, a gravity water bottle, and perhaps a fruit tree branch to chew and/or a salt licking stone.

BEDDING

Wood shavings are a popular choice for rabbit bedding, but avoid pine and cedar shavings as they have been linked to health problems in small animals. Buy wood shavings that are intended for use with pets (rather than buying from a lumberyard) to make sure that no chemicals are present which might be toxic for your pet. Pet stores also sell bedding made from wood pulp. Timothy hay is another good choice since rabbits enjoy eating it as well as sleeping in it.

An outdoor rabbit can have the same bedding as an indoor one during warm weather, but during a cold or rainy winter it will

CHOOSING THE RIGHT FLOORING

Due to their long fur, Angora rabbits need to be kept in a cage with a wire floor. This allows the rabbit's droppings and urine to fall through the floor onto a tray underneath. An Angora rabbit that is kept in an ordinary hutch will become very dirty, and its fur will get tangled and knotty. (For the same reason, the hay fed to an Angora should be tied to the side of the cage or kept in a hayrack.)

The Angora has heavily-furred feet, so a wire floor will not bother it. However, other breeds are best kept on an ordinary floor, covered with bedding, otherwise the wire floors cause discomfort and even injury. Slatted floors are a good option for all but the smallest rabbits (whose feet may become stuck between the slats). Otherwise, cover the wire floor with a piece of wood or a grass or sisal mat. Some people replace the wire floor with a single piece of linoleum.

need the extra protection of a thick layer of straw on top of the bedding. Rabbits can withstand very cold temperatures but they can't handle a wet or drafty hutch.

Never use newspaper as bedding for your rabbit. The rabbit will tear it to pieces, making a big mess, and the ink can be toxic. Pale-colored rabbits may also pick up ink stains from it.

FOOD BOWLS
The ideal food bowl is earthenware, heavy enough that the rabbit cannot tip it over, or a metal one which hooks onto the wire front of the rabbit hutch. Never use a plastic bowl—the rabbit will soon chew it to pieces, and may become ill if it swallows a piece of the plastic. (More on feeding in the next chapter.)

DRINKING BOTTLES
Most rabbits drink a fair amount of water, especially if they are not fed fresh, water-rich food, so clean water must be available at all times. The best method is to attach a gravity water bottle to the front or side of the hutch.

LITTER BOX
Most rabbits can be trained to use a litter box, although this does take some time and patience on your part. Begin by placing a small litter box in a corner of the cage. If you are using a

A gravity water bottle and a heavy earthenware or metal food bowl are essential items.

cage which is too small for a commercial litter box, a small glass baking dish may work as a substitute. (See Chapter 3.) Avoid using commercial cat litter products, especially clumping types that can get caught in a rabbit's feet. Organic litter products are preferable, such as those made from hay, oats, paper, or citrus. Cedar and pine shavings should not be used.

TOYS

Make sure toys are made of tough materials which cannot easily be chewed apart and that they don't have sharp edges. Safe alternatives include untreated wood blocks or cardboard, such as paper towel or toilet paper rolls. Place a few toys inside the cage for the rabbit to play with when you are not around.

The Outside Run

A run is an enclosure which can be placed on the ground so that the rabbit can safely enjoy the outdoors and nibble at the grass. A run can be purchased from a pet shop or be custom built. Sample plans are available at a number of rabbit-related sites on the Internet. The run must have a lid to prevent rabbits from jumping out, and a wire bottom to keep them from digging tunnels underneath. There should also be a covered area where the rabbit can take shelter from hot sun or rain. Some owners prefer outdoor pens, such as those used for dogs, but your rabbit may try to tunnel out. Keep an eye on your rabbit whenever it's outdoors to ensure its safety.

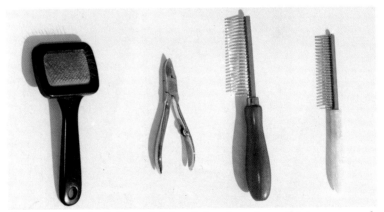

Grooming tools (left to right): slicker brush, nail trimmer, and metal combs.

Grooming Equipment

You'll need just a few grooming tools to keep your rabbit in excellent condition. (See Chapter 3 for grooming tips.)

NAIL CLIPPERS
All rabbits need their claws trimmed from time to time. Your local pet shop should be able to show you a selection of nail-clippers and give you advice on which will suit your needs.

COMBS
You'll need a fine-toothed metal comb like those made for cats. This will remove dead hairs easily from a shorthaired breed (especially when it's shedding) and put the finishing touches to a well-groomed longhaired rabbit. For a longhaired breed, you'll also need a metal comb with wider teeth to remove knots and to get through slightly matted fur.

SLICKER BRUSH
This is useful for both shorthaired and longhaired breeds. No other type of brush will get through the rabbit's dense fur.

Pet Carriers

Never attempt to transport a rabbit in a cardboard box. The rabbit can push its way through the lid, or even chew its way out. A proper pet carrier or traveling box is essential for trips to the vet and elsewhere. Plastic and metal carriers with handles are available, as well as soft carriers that look like luggage and folding crates for transporting multiple rabbits to a show.

GETTING YOUR BUNNY USED TO A CARRIER
Like most other small pets, rabbits aren't always keen on getting into a pet carrier. One way to keep the carrier familiar is to put the rabbit in it whenever you're cleaning the cage—and don't forget to offer some treats during its stay to make the association a pleasant one.

Traditional wooden carrying boxes are still used by some owners, while others prefer the more modern plastic carriers with wire doors. Make sure to provide your pet with a stable, non-slippery surface while he's in the carrier.

Other Useful Equipment

These are not essential for the well-being of the rabbit, but may make life a little easier for the owner.

RUBBER MAT
Use this to set the rabbit on while it is being groomed. Your pet will be calmer if he's not nervous about a slippery surface.

HAYRACK
A hayrack keeps hay from being soiled. You can buy one from a well-stocked pet shop or make one out of wire mesh.

BOTTLE BRUSH
Buy a brush designed to clean baby bottles. This will help keep your rabbit's water bottle free from algae, which quickly builds up, especially in warm weather.

PLASTIC PIPING OR VINYL TUBING
If you have an indoor rabbit, you'll need to cover electrical cables or wires so the rabbit can't chew on them. See Chapter 3 for more information on rabbit-proofing your home.

3

CARING FOR YOUR RABBIT

Feeding

You can keep your rabbit well-fed and in optimal health by providing three types of food, along with plenty of fresh water: a quality rabbit food (usually pellets), hay, and fresh plants.

Changing a rabbit's food needs to be done very gradually. A drastic change in diet can cause serious stomach upsets, and in extreme cases cause the death of your pet.

These days there are many brands of rabbit pellets available in pet stores.

PELLET FOODS

Almost all rabbit foods are "complete," which means that they include all the nutrients and vitamins a rabbit needs. A good pellet food will be about 14–16% protein with a fiber content of at least 18%.

Only use pet foods that are designed for rabbits! Do not use feed intended for other animals, such as hamsters or guinea pigs. These animals have different dietary needs than rabbits do, and the foods may actually be harmful to your rabbit.

SETTLING IN

When you get a new rabbit, find out what food it is used to and feed the same kind for at least a few days while the rabbit is settling in to its new home. If you want to feed your rabbit differently after that, make the change a gradual one. After several days, start to mix in small quantities of the new food with the old diet, about one quarter new food to three-quarters old food. Continue feeding this mixture for a few days, and observe the rabbit to see if the diet change is causing any problems, such as diarrhea. If all is well, gradually increase the proportion of new food until your rabbit is eating its new diet exclusively.

HAY

Most owners feed a daily diet that's about 80% pellets and 20% hay. Hay is essential for rabbits, providing the fiber they need to ensure proper digestive function. Purchase only dry, fresh-smelling hay and never feed wet or moldy hay to your rabbit. You can buy bagged hay from pet stores or obtain it by the bale from a farm or riding stable. Timothy hay is the best, but oat hay and mixed-grass hay can also be used. Do not feed alfalfa hay, except in small amounts as a rare treat, since it is too high in calories and calcium.

If you have to switch from one type of hay to another—especially if you have been feeding your rabbit old stored hay, and then buy freshly-cut green hay—make the change gradually to avoid digestive upset and diarrhea. Care should always be taken when feeding green hay if the rabbit is not used to it.

FRESH FOOD

Owners these days disagree as to how much fresh food to offer pet rabbits and some feel that with a complete rabbit food and hay, vegetables and and greens are not at all necessary.

Usually, however, the problem with feeding greens and vegetables lies in the types that are chosen, and how they are given. If a rabbit is used to eating just pellets and hay, it shouldn't be a surprise when diarrhea results after it's given fresh vegetables. This diarrhea is usually temporary, lasting just until the rabbit's digestive system adjusts to the new food. As with any other dietary change, offering fresh foods should be done gradually and with monitoring to see which, if any, cause stomach upset.

Recommended fresh foods for rabbits include dandelions, mustard greens, collard greens, endive, dill, parsley, romaine, cabbage, and carrot tops. Dark leafy greens are a better choice than light-colored ones. Avoid bibb and iceberg lettuce. Offer about a tablespoon of vegetables per day. You may also want to try tiny amounts of carrots, apples, pears, strawberries, squash, turnips and mangoes. Raw potatoes are also popular.

Do not feed bread, carbohydrates, or foods high in sugar or fat. For a rare treat, try a bit of banana, a few raisins, or a grape.

WATER
Water must always be available. In extreme weather, the water will need to be changed more frequently. Rabbits will not drink water that has warmed up in the sun nor will they lick ice for moisture if the water supply freezes. A rabbit that does not drink adequately will soon dehydrate and then cannot withstand the cold. Check the rabbit's drinking water regularly in cold weather and change it for fresh, preferably lukewarm, water as often as necessary.

QUANTITY
Normally, a grown rabbit will be quite happy if it is fed pellets once a day and has access to timothy hay at all times. The time of day you choose to feed pellets does not matter, but try to feed at the same time every day since rabbits like their routines. Nursing mothers (does) and youngsters under five months old need to be fed twice a day. If your rabbit appears to be very

PROTEIN REQUIREMENTS
The average pet rabbit needs a diet that is 14–16% protein. If the diet contains more protein than this the rabbit will quickly become overweight and may develop serious health problems, such as fatty liver or kidney failure. However, there are some situations where higher protein levels are beneficial: for does that are pregnant or nursing, for rabbits who are kept outside during the winter (the added protein helps them keep warm), and for young rabbits of large breeds, such as French Lops, until they are fully grown.

hungry, increase the daily amount of food. If the rabbit starts to become fat, reduce the amount of pellets you're feeding. Not surprisingly, large rabbits eat more food than small ones do.

Cleaning the Hutch

One of your most important tasks is to keep your rabbit's hutch clean. A soiled hutch smells bad, attracts flies and maggots, and serves as a breeding ground for bacteria.

How often you clean the hutch depends on the size of the rabbit, the size of the hutch, and how naturally clean the rabbit is—if the rabbit is litter-trained or restricts its toileting to one corner, you can clean that area frequently and the rest of the cage less often. A large hutch with a small rabbit will not need as much cleaning as a same size hutch with a larger rabbit.

When cleaning the hutch, begin by putting your rabbit in a pet carrier or another cage. Next, use a dustpan to scoop up soiled bedding and a brush to sweep everything up from the hutch floor. A paint scraper is useful for removing tough dirt. When the hutch is clean, fill it with new bedding. Every six months or so, disinfect the hutch with a non-toxic liquid cleaner. Always disinfect the hutch or cage before moving a new rabbit into it, especially if the former occupant has died.

Grooming

The safest way to handle your rabbit when it needs grooming is to place it on a table on a non-slip rubber mat so that it will feel secure. To groom the rabbit's stomach and legs, sit down and hold the rabbit in your lap, laying it on its back.

SHORTHAIRED RABBITS
Shorthaired rabbits don't need regular grooming since their coats aren't long enough to get matted. However, when it is in heavy molt (i.e. when it is shedding, which usually happens in the spring and autumn) you can help the rabbit remove the old dead coat by grooming it with a fine metal comb or a slicker brush. If you use a slicker brush, take care not to scratch the rabbit's skin with the metal bristles.

Grooming a longhaired rabbit: Begin by placing the rabbit on a non-slip mat on a table. Then use a wide-toothed comb to comb the back and sides.

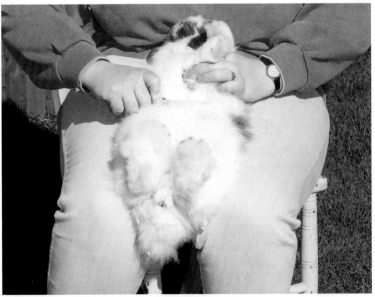

When grooming the areas underneath, sit down with the rabbit laid on its back on your lap.

LONGHAIRED RABBITS

Longhaired rabbits need regular grooming all year round. Most longhaired rabbits will have grown their full coat by the age of six months. Grooming gets easier then, as the very woolly baby fur can be quite difficult to care for. Angora rabbits need to be groomed several times a week.

When grooming a longhaired rabbit, start with a wide-toothed comb and carefully comb through all the fur, gently picking out any knots. Use a pair of round-tip scissors to very carefully cut out the worst knots. When you have gone through the coat with a wide-toothed comb, switch to a fine-toothed comb and go over the whole rabbit once again. Pay special attention to the areas behind the ears, on the chest, and the stomach. Always be very careful when grooming because a rabbit's delicate skin will easily tear if it is pulled too hard.

TRIMMING CLAWS

Rabbit claws must be trimmed on a regular basis—about every other month. All you need is a suitable pair of nail trimmers. Sit down and hold the rabbit firmly in your lap, or ask someone to hold the rabbit while you cut its claws. A pale-colored rabbit will normally have white claws. These are very easy to trim since the pink quick (the blood supply) is visible. If your rabbit has dark claws, shine a flashlight under the claw so you can see the quick. Trim the claw, but not too close to the quick. If you cut into the quick, the claw will bleed. It's a good idea to keep a styptic pencil on hand to stop the bleeding. These are available at your local pharmacy.

Don't forget to trim the dewclaws on the front legs. Situated an inch or so up on the rabbit's leg, these do not wear down naturally, and can become severely overgrown if they are neglected, even to the point of piercing the skin on the leg.

If you are not comfortable doing the trimming, ask your vet or groomer to walk you through the process. Likewise, your rabbit may not be comfortable with the process. A struggling rabbit can injure itself, so if it is trying to get away, put the nail trimming off to another day and then try again.

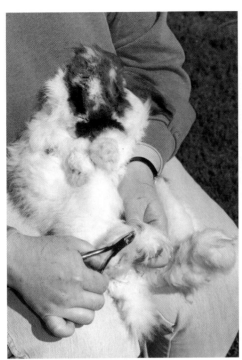

When trimming the nails, hold your rabbit firmly but gently. Ask for someone to help you hold the rabbit if you find it difficult to do this task by yourself.

Using nail trimmers, trim the tip from each claw. Be careful not to cut into the quick.

Nail trimming needs to be done approximately every other month.

Additional Care

Check the rabbit's ears when you groom him, but generally you do not need to do any other ear care unless an infection is present. Also check the rabbit's teeth—sometimes they become overgrown and need special attention. (This is discussed under "Malocclusion" in Chapter 4.)

There are only very rare instances when you should consider bathing a rabbit, such as when it is sick and has soiled itself badly (and even so, call your vet first for advice). Immersing a rabbit in water can cause it to go into shock.

The best way to keep your rabbit clean is to ensure that it doesn't get dirty in the first place. The key to this is keeping the rabbit's hutch clean. A healthy rabbit will lick itself several times a day to keep its coat clean. Small stains can be wiped off the rabbit's coat with a damp cloth or unscented baby wipe.

Handling Your Rabbit

A rabbit that is handled in the wrong way, or is not used to handling, will panic and can inflict nasty scratches by kicking with its hind legs. The best way to handle a new rabbit that has not yet had time to get to know you is by firmly gripping the scruff, just behind the rabbit's ears, with one hand, and then lifting it up, while supporting its hindquarters with the other hand. Handled in this way, the rabbit will feel secure and is not likely to kick or struggle. Once out of the hutch, place the rabbit against your chest, with one hand supporting the hindquarters, the other across its back.

If you do not feel confident enough to carry the rabbit like this just yet, place it on a low table and gently stroke it. It helps to place a rubber mat on the table, as the rabbit's furry feet are likely to slip. A tame rabbit can be picked up by placing one hand underneath it, just behind the front legs, and the other hand supporting the hindquarters. If not too large, the rabbit can be carried around sitting on your arm, as long as you support it with the other arm. Under no circumstances should a rabbit be picked up by its ears! This is very painful and terrifies the rabbit.

To hold a tame rabbit, place one hand under the front legs and support the hindquarters with your other hand.

When you have just acquired a new rabbit, let it settle in for a couple of days—just feed it and otherwise leave it alone. After a couple of days, you can start to get the rabbit used to you. The more you handle it, the tamer it will become. To gain the rabbit's confidence, start by offering it small food treats from your hand, such as a

When you are taming your rabbit and getting used to each other, place it on a table and stroke it gently.

dandelion leaf or bit of banana. The rabbit soon learns that your presence means food and will get excited when you come near the hutch. Most rabbits love to have their foreheads scratched. Rabbits that are used to this sort of treatment will even run up to your hand and rub their heads against it.

When handling a new rabbit outside the hutch, place it on a low table to start with, in case the rabbit panics and jumps off. Once the rabbit is used to being petted on a table, you can hold it on your lap. Bear in mind that rabbits do not like being carried around; even a very tame rabbit will protest eventually. Your rabbit will prefer sitting on your lap for a while or running around the room. If you get down to ground level, you will find it is easier to interact with your rabbit.

Litter Training

Some rabbits are litter trained quite easily, others require more of an investment of time and patience. Occasional "accidents" may still occur. Fortunately, rabbit droppings are small and easy to clean up! Begin by placing a small litter box inside the rabbit's cage. Cat litter is not the best option for rabbits since they tend to nibble on the litter material, so avoid that in favor of organic litter materials made of paper, grasses, or citrus. These are highly absorbent and help reduce urine odors. You can also use hay in the litter box though it needs to be changed more frequently than the other materials. Do not use cedar or pine shavings as these pose health risks for small animals.

The rabbit's instincts help with litter training: a rabbit does not want to soil areas where it eats or sleeps. You can also give it some hints by placing its droppings in the litter box, even to the point of transferring a few old droppings to the fresh litter when you clean out the box. Keep the rabbit primarily in the cage until it understands what the litter box is for.

As you begin letting the rabbit spend time out of its cage, keep it in a small area where it can quickly return to the litter box when it needs to. As you give it more freedom to roam, you may want to provide additional litter boxes, usually in the corners of rooms. The typical rabbit is not willing to travel far to find a litter box. You may want to use covered litter boxes outside of the cage, or ones with higher sides, to confine the mess.

If your rabbit frequently tries to urinate or defecate in a particular corner of the room, put a litter box there. Placing a food bowl or treats there is another option, so that the rabbit associates that spot with eating and not toileting.

Praise your rabbit and offer a treat when you notice him using the litter box. Never punish a pet for mistakes in toilet training. Young rabbits in particular don't have the attention span it takes to achieve total litter training—it may take several months or up to a year to complete the process.

Spaying/neutering is also important for litter training success. Otherwise, as hormones become more active, male and female rabbits want to spray and urinate to mark their territories.

Changes in routine which seem small to you can be distressing to your rabbit and cause some forgetfulness about using the litter box. This often happens when other rabbits or pets are introduced into the household. Even when life is calm for your rabbit, don't be surprised if he or she leaves a few droppings near the cage—this is not a failure of litter training, just your rabbit's way of claiming its "home" territory.

KEEPING ODORS UNDER CONTROL

Frequent cleaning of the rabbit's cage and litter box are essential for its health and the atmosphere of your home. Change litter daily and rinse the box out with water. For deeper cleaning, wash the box with a weak solution of water and white vinegar. Do not use bleach or household cleaners.

If a rabbit who has been using the litter box successfully starts to have problems, this can be a sign of stress or a health problem such as a urinary infection. Pay attention when cleaning the cage—changes in urine odor, color, or quantity can indicate a health problem such as a bladder infection. Changes in the consistency or color of droppings are also worth noting and you should contact your vet if you think there's reason for concern. Otherwise, repeat the steps you used to litter train the animal in the first place, confining it mostly to the cage until it starts using the litter box again.

Rabbit-Proofing Your Home

If you're going to let your rabbit loose in the house, you need to make the home (or parts of it) safe for your rabbit to explore. Chewing and digging are natural, instinctive rabbit behaviors which can be managed but not eliminated. Rabbits need time to learn proper behavior, just as small children do. Start by rabbit-proofing one room where the rabbit will be allowed out of his cage for supervised playtimes.

1. **ELECTRICAL WIRES MUST BE WELL-HIDDEN OR COVERED.**
   Chewing on electrical cords, phone wires, etc., holds a dangerous attraction for rabbits, and biting through the cords can electrocute them. Move the cords or hide them behind furniture. Otherwise, enclose wires in PVC or plastic tubing, available at hardware and electronics stores. Some types come already split, making it easy to wrap cords. Hard plastic molding is another option. You may need to try more than one method before you find the one that works best.

2. **SAFELY STORE CHEMICALS AND MEDICATIONS.**
   Never leave household cleaners, chemicals, or medications (for humans or animals)—or even the empty containers—

RABBIT CARE

THE RABBIT'S CAGE IS HIS CASTLE.
Rabbits who feel stressed are likely to begin marking
their territory with urine or droppings. Help prevent this
by remembering that the cage is not just a place to
confine and control your rabbit—it is the rabbit's
home and he needs to feel secure there.

Try not to reach in and grab the rabbit to take him out.
Instead, as much as possible, open the door and let him
choose when to come out. Likewise, try not to put the rabbit directly back into the cage, but set him in front of it and
let him enter. Don't make him feel like going into the cage is
a punishment. It's also a good idea to let your rabbit out of
the cage while you clean it so he isn't upset by you moving
things around and being "in his space." Some owners train
their rabbits that a particular word or phrase means
that it's time to go back into the cage.

where the rabbit can get to them. Even ingesting a small
amount can be fatal.

3. **PREVENT DROWNING.**
   Rabbits love to jump! Close toilet seat lids and keep the
   rabbit away from sinks, bathtubs, mop buckets, etc.

4. **PLACE HOUSEPLANTS OUT OF REACH OR OUT OF THE ROOM.**
   Many plants, including bulbs of all kinds, ivy, aloe, yucca,
   philodendrons, and poinsettia are toxic to rabbits.

5. **ADDITIONAL SAFETY STEPS: BETTER SAFE THAN SORRY!**
   Keep cabinets and drawers closed. If the rabbit is chewing
   on furniture, either cover the legs of the furniture or spray
   bitter apple (sold in pet stores) to make the item taste bad.
   Let family members know the rabbit is on the loose so that
   no one accidentally sits or steps on him. Be careful about
   things like recliner chairs which can entrap small pets. Use
   baby gates to help define areas that are off-limits.

6. **PROVIDE BUNNY WITH APPROPRIATE THINGS TO CHEW ON.**
   Bored pets get into mischief. Provide "chew toys" such as
   untreated wood blocks or branches, cardboard boxes, grass
   mats, untreated wicker baskets, etc.

Rabbit Behavior

Pet rabbits have a range of behavior patterns in common with their wild cousins:

CHIN-RUBBING
The rabbit has scent glands on its chin. By rubbing against things (and people), the rabbit deposits scent to identify its belongings to other rabbits. Humans cannot smell this scent.

SPRAYING
The buck rabbit may spray urine over his hutch, his food bowl, and anything else within reach as a way of establishing his ownership. Neutering resolves much of this behavior.

LASHING OUT WITH FORELEGS
The rabbit springs forward and aggressively lashes out with its forelegs as if to say, "Get out of my space!" This behavior is often seen in does, especially when they are nursing.

CIRCLING
The buck rabbit keeps going around in circles, making low, purring noises. This means he is looking for a doe to mate.

ROLLING OVER
If your rabbit rolls over on its back, looking almost dead, with all four legs stretched out, don't be alarmed. The rabbit does this when it is feeling thoroughly content and happy!

BROODY DOES
The doe rabbit runs around with tufts of hay or any other kind of bedding in her mouth, as she attempts to build a nest. This behavior obviously also occurs in pregnant does.

HIGH-PITCHED SCREAMING
This is the rabbit's way of expressing extreme fear.

HEY, BUNNY!
Use your rabbit's name on all occasions, perhaps giving a small treat at the same time. The rabbit will soon realize the name refers to him and will be quick to respond because you've created a pleasant association.

HEALTH CARE

This list is a general guide to the most common health issues affecting pet rabbits. Many of these ailments can be prevented by maintaining good nutrition and clean housing.

Coccidiosis

Coccidiosis is a parasitic infection which can be fatal, especially in young rabbits. Most healthy rabbits are hosts to at least a few of these parasites, the eggs of which are passed out in the rabbit's feces. If the right conditions are present, such as warm and humid weather, the eggs become infected. If they are eaten by the rabbit, or picked up when the rabbit licks its feet or fur, they develop into parasites that attack the rabbit's intestine. The rabbit may suffer from diarrhea, weight loss, jaundice, or develop a distended stomach or "pot belly." If caught early enough, your vet can treat this with sulfa drugs or other medications, but the most important way to control Coccidiosis is to make sure that the rabbit's hutch is kept clean, especially during hot weather.

Worms

Roundworms are the most common type in rabbits, but tapeworms also occur. A rabbit may be infected by eating grass that contains eggs or catch worms from another rabbit. Symptoms include pot belly, poor coat and, in youngsters, poor growth. Sometimes worms can actually be seen around the rabbit's tail. The treatment is a mild liquid wormer, such as those used for kittens. Ask your vet for advice on dosage. Wormers bought from a veterinarian are usually safer and more effective than those bought over the counter.

External Parasites

If your rabbit appears to be scratching all the time, suspect parasites such as mites. You can usually see these on the rabbit's fur around the face and neck. Mites are usually brought in via infested hay or picked up from another animal. The rabbit can be sprayed with an insecticidal spray, or treated orally or by injection with parasite cures. Never use a flea dip or bathe the rabbit. Ask your vet for treatment advice.

Ringworm

Ringworm is a very infectious fungus, and can be transferred between animals and humans. In humans, it manifests as itchy round red patches. On rabbits, the symptoms are fur loss and lots of white dandruff, especially on the neck and back. Ringworm can be difficult to get rid of, since the spores can spread to the rabbit's bedding, hutch, the owner's clothes, etc. The rabbit will need medication prescribed by a vet.

Abscesses

If you find a hard or soft swelling on a rabbit's body, it's usually an abscess, a wound (usually from a bite) which has become infected. If the abscess has not started to drain on its own, take the animal to the vet so the abscess can be lanced. You'll need to squeeze out any pus that occurs in the next few days. In severe cases, antibiotics may be needed. It's important to treat wounds promptly to prevent abscesses from occurring.

HEALTH CARE

Vent Disease ("Hutch Burn")

Rabbits with sore and swollen genitalia may have vent disease. If the rabbit has been licking itself, there may be blisters on the mouth and around the nose. Vent disease occurs when rabbits are kept in dirty hutches and is more common in does than in bucks. A seemingly healthy buck may be a carrier of the disease and pass it on to the doe when mating. You'll need to see the vet in order to get treatment for this.

Rhinitis ("Snuffles")

Rhinitis, the disease commonly known as "snuffles" or "sniffles," is extremely contagious and can easily be fatal. The rabbit sneezes, has a runny nose and eyes, and appears sickly. The fur on the inside of the front legs becomes matted as the rabbit uses these to wipe its nose. Pasteurella bacteria is often the source of the illness and antibiotics will be needed.

It is vital to isolate infected rabbits from healthy ones to prevent a further spread. Keep sick rabbits in separate cages at least ten feet away from others. The disease is spread by airborne nasal secretions, so rabbits can become infected even if not in direct contact with sick ones. To be extra careful, make a practice of isolating any new rabbit, or ones that have visited a show, for a few days to make sure they're healthy.

Constipation

A constipated rabbit appears lethargic and has an extended belly. Suspect constipation if you see these symptoms and note a lack of droppings in the rabbit's hutch. Lack of water is a common cause of constipation, or the rabbit may have been eating straw instead of hay. In mild cases, it is usually enough to feed the rabbit some fresh food, such as carrot or lettuce.

ALTERED RABBITS LIVE LONGER.
By spaying or neutering your pet rabbit, you increase his or her probable life span. Females that are not spayed often die of uterine or ovarian cancer while non-neutered males are prone to testicular cancer.

(Lettuce should not be fed under other circumstances.) If the rabbit does not want to eat, a few drops of paraffin oil or corn oil will usually do the trick. If nothing works, contact your vet.

Diarrhea ("Scours")

A rabbit can develop diarrhea from stress, dietary changes such as eating too much fresh food, or illness. Feed the rabbit dry food only, rabbit pellets and hay, until the problem clears up. Make sure plenty of water is available as a rabbit with diarrhea can become dehydrated quickly. In severe cases, a few drops of liquid charcoal may help. Call your vet for other suggestions.

NOTE: Do not confuse diarrhea with the soft droppings that are passed by rabbits during the night. These soft droppings are perfectly normal. They contain a high amount of vitamin B, and the rabbit needs to eat them to benefit from the vitamin.

Intestinal Blockages and Hairballs

Unlike cats, rabbits can't vomit to get rid of hairballs, so these can cause a dangerous blockage of the intestines, especially during peak shedding times. Blockages may also occur if the rabbit has eaten non-digestible items. Consider intestinal blockage if the rabbit has little appetite and is losing weight despite a bloated stomach. With a blockage, droppings get smaller and may contain hairs.

Offer fresh foods and hay. If this doesn't quickly bring relief, contact your vet for treatment. The best prevention is to feed plenty of hay and a small serving of greens each day.

Bloat

A rabbit's belly can also become distended from a build-up of gas, usually due to overfeeding of green food. The rabbit huddles in a corner of its hutch, not wishing to eat or move. Consult a vet as soon as possible. The rabbit will die if this condition is not treated properly.

Malocclusion

Sometimes a rabbit's teeth grow misaligned. Since the upper and lower teeth do not meet, the teeth do not wear down naturally and grow too long. Eventually the rabbit finds it impossible to eat. Clipping the teeth is necessary, often on a regular basis. See your vet. You may be able to perform the procedure on your own after getting the vet's instruction. This is often an inherited condition, so these rabbits should not be bred from.

Myxomatosis

This is a highly fatal viral disease. It was deliberately brought into the British and Australian populations of wild rabbits to reduce their numbers. Affected rabbits show swollen eyelids, with swellings at the base of the ears and around the nose, sometimes also at other parts of the body. Death usually occurs within a few days. There is a vaccine available though it is not widely available in the U.S. The best prevention is mosquito control, since the disease is spread by insect bites.

Rabbit Viral Hemorrhagic Disease

Rabbit Viral Hemorrhagic Disease (RVHD) has killed hundreds of thousands of rabbits in Europe. Two outbreaks have been confirmed in the U.S. since 2000. RVHD is extremely infectious and and can be carried on items such as clothing, and even on frozen dead rabbits. Symptoms include lethargy, loss of appetite, spasms or sudden death. However, disease onset is so fast, no symptoms may be noticed. Death can occur within 48 hours. A vaccine is available in some countries where the disease is more common, but not yet in the U.S.

IS THERE BLOOD IN THE URINE?
Many rabbit owners are alarmed to see that their pets are passing bright red urine, but this is most often just a red tint that comes from plants that the rabbit has eaten. If it were blood in the urine, it would show as specks of red. Any time you suspect blood in the urine, especially if other symptoms are present, contact your vet for advice.

5

BREEDING RABBITS

Whether to Breed

No breeding plan should be undertaken lightly. Here are three common reasons why people consider breeding rabbits:

TO PRODUCE A LITTER FROM A BELOVED PET
Do you know how to look after the pregnant mother, and how to care for the doe and her litter? Is your pet doe a good enough specimen to be bred from? Pure-bred animals are more likely to find a good permanent home than are cross-breeds. In either case, make sure that both the doe and buck are healthy and of good temperament. You may end up with five or more babies to find homes for. What will you do with the ones you can't keep? It is unlikely the local pet shop will take them and it can be difficult to find good homes for rabbits—as animal shelters and rabbit rescue organizations will readily tell you.

TO PRODUCE QUALITY RABBITS FOR SHOWING
Are you prepared to make a significant financial investment, both in breeding stock and in caring for the animals? You will also need to do a lot of research—reading, talking to other breeders, attending shows—before you get started.

Always start off with a doe that is of good quality. You will not get far by breeding from mediocre stock. If you want to interest other rabbit fanciers in buying your stock, they must be of as good quality as possible. Inevitably you will get youngsters in each litter that are not quite up to show standard, and you must plan for these as well. What will you do with them?

TO MAKE MONEY RAISING RABBITS

If you plan to breed rabbits to make money, then I suggest that you forget the whole thing. There are only two ways to make money out of rabbits. One way is to sell good, show-quality rabbits, bred from show-winning stock, to other breeders and exhibitors. Achieving this standard on a regular basis takes years of dedication and will cost you a lot of money. The other way is to breed rabbits for meat, which is a subject that does not belong in a book about pet rabbits.

Before you decide to breed from your doe, you must be confident that she's a good specimen of her breed.

The Right Age for Breeding

Most doe rabbits can be mated for the first time at five to six months of age. A younger, immature doe may not look after her litter properly. Large breeds, such as the French Lop, need longer to mature, so with large breeds it is better to wait until about nine months of age.

A doe must not be older than twelve months when her first litter is born. Before this age her pelvis will be soft and can stretch when giving birth. If the doe has not had a litter by twelve months, the pelvic bone will have fused in position and cannot open properly for her to give birth.

Does of small breeds, such as the Netherland Dwarf, can often continue breeding until they are three or four years of age. In other breeds, does usually retire from breeding at the age of three. A doe that is getting past her prime will produce babies that are fewer in number and smaller in size, and more that are stillborn. These are signs it is time to retire the doe. Bucks can be used for breeding from the age of about four to five months right up to five years.

Mating

The first rule regarding the mating of rabbits is that it should never be done in the doe's hutch. The doe will defend her hutch from intruders and attack any visiting buck.

Unlike other small animals such as guinea pigs and hamsters, female rabbits can mate successfully even when not in heat. The act of mating triggers the doe to ovulate. However, a doe actually comes into heat about every seventeen to twenty-one days and is more willing to mate at those times. A doe in heat will wiggle her tail when her back is touched and crouch low on her forelegs with her tail stuck up in the air, ready for the buck to mate her.

When your doe is in heat and willing to be mated, put her in the buck's hutch. Mating usually takes place fairly promptly. Most breeds need strict supervision to prevent the doe from attacking the buck after mating. Allow the buck to mate the doe at least once or twice more to increase the chance of pregnancy. Not many bucks will mate more than four or five times, so after this remove the doe to her own hutch.

Is the Doe Pregnant?

The gestation period for a rabbit is 28–34 days, with 30–32 days being the average. It can be difficult to tell whether the doe is pregnant or not, as the vast majority do not look pregnant. An experienced breeder or vet will be able to feel the rabbit fetuses inside the doe after approximately three weeks by carefully palpating the abdomen. This should never be attempted by a novice as it can harm the unborn babies if not done correctly. Your best bet is to wait thirty-four days from the day of mating. If nothing has happened by then, the doe was not pregnant.

Pregnancy

The first sign that the doe is pregnant is when you see her preparing a nest for her litter. Most does start nesting a couple of days before the litter is due, but some don't begin until a few hours before the birth. The nest will usually be built in a corner of the rabbit's hutch, and it will consist of hay and/or straw, lined with fur which the doe will pluck from her own abdomen.

The nest is crucial since babies born or kept outside a warm nest will be too cold to survive. Some does are better nest-builders than others. A good doe will make a huge nest, and pluck so much fur from her belly—and possibly front legs as well—that she will be partially bald. This is perfectly normal and the fur will soon grow back.

Other does pluck their fur but leave it scattered around the hutch. If this happens, collect all the fur and place it in the nest. You may also want to add some soft hay. Some breeders like to give their nursing doe a nest box—a box made of wood, just large enough for the doe to sit in. A nest box has pros and cons. It helps keep the babies in one place and can easily be removed from the hutch so that the litter can be inspected. The disadvantage is that any baby that happens to fall out of the nest box will not be picked up by the doe and put back into the nest. If this happens, the baby will die if you do not find it in time.

PHANTOM PREGNANCIES

If the doe starts nesting two or three weeks after mating, you can usually assume that she is not pregnant. False or phantom pregnancies are very common in rabbits. The doe will believe that she is pregnant—sometimes when she has not even been mated—and she will build a nest and will generally behave as though she were pregnant.

Preparing for the Birth

Since you can't always know for certain whether the doe is pregnant, assume that she is. Around twenty-seven days after the mating, clean out the the doe's hutch and fill it with plenty of hay, wood shavings, and straw. It's essential that the doe has a good supply of nesting material. Make sure that food and water are available at all times, as a thirsty or hungry doe may occasionally kill and eat her babies.

The Birth

Most domestic rabbits give birth during the night or early
morning when no one is around. It is rare to see any signs of
the birth, such as blood. The doe usually covers her litter so
well that it is impossible to see whether the nest is full or
empty without reaching into it. Keep a close eye on the doe, or
remove her from the hutch, when you do this as she may
attack any intruder after the litter has been born.

If you can feel babies in the nest, leave them alone for the first
couple of days. Make sure the doe has as much peace and quiet
as possible during this time. A nursing doe that is disturbed
may kill her babies in a sort of misguided attempt to protect
them. Some does will kill their babies if they are disturbed,
others will scatter the nest and babies in all directions, which
is just as bad since the babies will die from cold if they are not
discovered very soon.

Inspecting the Litter

Approximately three days after the birth, try to inspect the litter. Always remove the doe from the hutch first. Before handling the babies, it is a good idea to rub your hands in some
soiled bedding from the hutch to mask your scent. Gently part
the nest and look at the babies inside. Quite commonly, there
will be one or two dead babies which must be removed. Dead
babies are usually found buried right at the bottom of the nest.

One or two babies are usually much smaller than their littermates, perhaps only a third of the size of their siblings. Such
babies are termed runts and they usually die since they are not
strong enough to compete for food with their larger littermates.

Normal litter size for a small doe, such as a Netherland Dwarf,
is two to four babies, though it can vary from one to six. Does
of these small breeds can usually cope well with up to six
babies. Slightly larger breeds, such as the Dwarf Lop, normally
have litters consisting of three to five babies, although numbers
as high as nine can occur. Giant breeds usually have large litters, with anything from five to twelve being quite common.

BREEDING

Caring for the Litter

Rabbit babies remain in their nest for ten to fourteen days. During this time, you can inspect them every day if the doe is not upset by this. Do very little hutch cleaning during this time so that you don't distress the doe; just remove the worst soiled areas and replace the bedding. Wait for three weeks before doing a full cleaning.

A doe needs more food than normal while she is nursing. Feeding twice a day is a good idea and supplements such as a bran mash every day will help to keep her milk supply going. You are not likely to see the doe nursing her litter because rabbits only nurse their young a couple of times in a twenty-four hour period, most often at night.

Rabbits are born without fur, but usually have a hint of pigmentation. You can distinguish between pale and dark-colored animals immediately after birth. After a day or two, more pigmentation will appear and it will be easy to tell if a baby is self-colored or broken-marked (spotted). After about a week the babies are fully covered with short fur, though it may not be in its final coloring. For example, an agouti-colored baby rabbit looks more black than brown. At around the age of two weeks it should be possible to tell what colors the babies actually are.

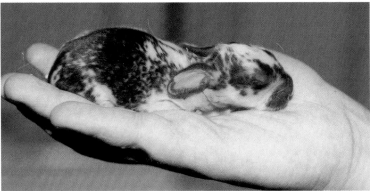

Although he's only a few days old, we can tell this French Lop baby is going to be spotted.

As you can see from the litter of French Lops in this nest box, rabbits are born without any fur.

The same litter of French Lops, now two weeks old.

Rabbit mothers usually take good care of their young.

Babies start to leave the nest and explore once their eyes have opened, at about ten to fourteen days of age. Handle them regularly to get them used to people. Increase the food supply when the babies leave the nest and be sure to use a food bowl which the babies can easily access.

Babies should be left with their mother for at least five, and preferably six, weeks after birth. By that time, the doe will start to chase them away and nip them if they come too close. Remove all babies from the mother at the same time and keep them together in a separate hutch before selling them. In this way, the change from living with the mother to living on their own is a more gradual one.

The doe should have time to rest before being mated again. If she is thin with hardly any fur on her belly, she will need a much longer period of rest than if she remained in good condition. Breeding a doe more than three times a year is usually discouraged.

SHOWING RABBITS

Showing rabbits is a hobby, just like showing dogs or any other animal. It enables you to make new friends with the same interest as you. If you want to breed pure-bred rabbits, showing is a must since it establishes the good points and bad points of your rabbits, which is vital information for your breeding program. Showing (and especially winning) also establishes your breeding program in the eyes of potential buyers. Even if you are not a breeder, there is a wealth of knowledge among the exhibitors and judges at rabbit shows, and you will learn a great deal about rabbits and rabbit-keeping.

How to Start Showing

In America, the organization that sets the standards and rules for rabbit shows is the American Rabbit Breeders Association (ARBA). The best place to get started is the ARBA website: www.arba.net. ARBA publishes the essential guide for showing pure-bred rabbits, *Standard of Perfection,* which contains information on standards for each sanctioned breed. This and many other helpful guides for rabbit owners are available for purchase at the ARBA website. If you are serious about showing rabbits, you should become a member of this organization. There are also regional clubs as well as clubs focusing on particular breeds, all of which may sponsor shows and offer other benefits to their members.

The best way of getting involved in the show scene is to start by visiting a rabbit show as a spectator. This way you can watch the procedures and you will, no doubt, find club members and

Each rabbit is examined individually by the judge. Your rabbit should be used to being handled if you intend to show him.

exhibitors who are happy to answer your questions. Show dates are listed on the ARBA website and in their official magazine for members, *Domestic Rabbits.*

Rabbits do not have to be pedigreed (i.e. with proof of ancestry for four generations) or pure-bred in order to be shown, but must be representative of an ARBA-sanctioned breed and color.

All rabbits entered in shows must have a tattoo in their left ear for identification. As the owner, you get to choose the letters and numbers to be used in this tattoo. You can buy a tattooing kit and do this yourself, have it done by a rabbit breeder, or pay a small fee and have it done at a show.

When you have chosen a show to enter, the listing on the ARBA calendar will provide contact information for the show secretary. Write or e-mail to ask for an information packet or show catalog—this will give you all the details about how to enter, the rules of the show, etc.

The entry form will ask for information about the rabbits you are entering: ear number (tattooed in the left ear), breed (for example, Holland Lop), variety (color and marking, as specified by ARBA; for example, sable or black), class (junior or senior—rabbits under six months of age are usually juniors, but this varies by breed and weight limits are also a factor), and sex (buck or doe). Make sure you send in your entry form by the deadline. Entry fees are usually small—just a few dollars per rabbit. Some shows offer monetary prizes, but these too are quite small.

Preparing Your Rabbit for the Show

How much show preparation your rabbit will need depends on the breed and color of the rabbit. Any longhaired breed will obviously need careful grooming before the show. Make sure that the fur is completely free of knots. Shorthaired breeds usually don't need grooming, other than a quick wipe-down with your hands to make the fur shine. If you are showing a white rabbit, make sure that it is as clean as possible, without any stains (the only way to ensure this is to keep the rabbit's hutch as clean as possible so that the white fur will not get stained). Also make sure nails are properly trimmed.

Other than this, the main preparation your rabbits will need is to be comfortable being handled so that they will not be frightened when the judges pick them up for examination.

The Day of the Show

Try to arrive at the show at least half an hour before judging is due to commence. You will need this time to settle your rabbit and do some final grooming.

Different shows have different procedures, but usually the first thing you will do upon arrival at the show hall is to report to the show secretary that you have arrived and to pay your entry fees.

The judge must be familiar with the distinguishing characteristics of each breed. At the end of the show, judges may meet to select the top prize, Best in Show.

Then find the area where your breed will be judged and set up close by so that you will hear when your rabbit's class is called. You will carry the rabbit to the judging table at that point and place him in the appropriate box.

Judging Procedures

The judge will examine each rabbit in turn, making notes on its good and bad points, how closely it conforms to the breed standard in use, and then will compare the rabbits entered against each other. Rabbits are judged on condition, color and marking, fur or wool, and general body type.

You may stand near the judging table and listen to the comments as the judging proceeds. Do not talk about your rabbit, though, since the judge is not supposed to know which rabbits belong to which owners.

After the judging has been completed, each rabbit will be issued a signed score card, which will state how many points (out of a given maximum) your rabbit has gained, in each separate section, such as color, ears, etc., and an overall total. The card will also state how many rabbits were entered in the class and where your rabbit placed. Full show rules can be obtained from the American Rabbit Breeders Association.

Remember that even though the rabbits are being judged against an established standard, the process is still a subjective one. It's not that unusual for a rabbit to win at one show and place low at the next. Different judges may apply the standards in slightly different ways.

Also remember...

...that your rabbit is first and foremost a pet and friend—not simply a show animal. No matter the outcome of the judging, your rabbit will always need and deserve the care and attention of a treasured companion and valuable member of your family.